CW01672455

To

Dear Mark & Hannah
and family

With much love and

Best Wishes

at this Season

& throughout the New Year

as the Lord may be pleased

to spare you all

25th December 2021

# WILLIAM TYNDALE
# ON PRIESTS AND PREACHERS,
# WITH NEW LIGHT ON HIS EARLY CAREER

# WILLIAM TYNDALE
## ON PRIESTS AND PREACHERS

---

WITH NEW LIGHT ON HIS EARLY CAREER

ANDREW J. BROWN

INSCRIPTOR IMPRINTS
LONDON
1996

First published in 1996 by Inscriptor Imprints,
PO Box 10926, London, SE18 7ZB, England.

ISBN 0 9528271 0 7

Printed and bound in Great Britain by Biddles Ltd.,
Woodbridge Road, Guildford, GU1 1DA.

# CONTENTS

Acknowledgments vi

Introduction 7

1. Tyndale's Origins 8

2. Tyndale's Ordination 12

3. Tyndale at Oxford 26

4. Early Narratives of Tyndale's Life 37

5. Tyndale's Views on Priests and Preachers 42

Abbreviations 72

Notes 73

Index 76

# ACKNOWLEDGMENTS

Thanks are due to several institutions for assistance given in the course of preparing this book, in particular the County Record Office of Hereford, the Guildhall Library in London, and the Oxford University Archives, by whose courtesy it has been possible to publish extracts from the manuscript registers in their keeping. Help has also been gratefully received from the Gloucestershire Record Office, the British Library, the Bodleian Library, the Doctor Williams' Library, St. Paul's Cathedral Library, and the University of London Institute of Historical Research.

# INTRODUCTION

The story of William Tyndale, his translation of the first New Testament ever to be printed in the English language, his leading role as a religious reformer, and his death as a martyr in 1536, is well known. His life has been the subject of several biographies, his writings have been analysed and edited, and the five hundredth anniversary of his birth has been duly celebrated. There are, however, certain aspects of his career which are capable of being further clarified from contemporary documents. The first part of the present study will examine the evidence relating to Tyndale's birth and upbringing, his studies at Oxford university, and the various stages of his ordination to the priesthood.

The second part of this short book is an anthology of Tyndale's views on the clergy, and the role of the Christian preacher. Although he was a polished product of the ecclesiastical and educational "system" of those days, his new understanding of the Bible and the influence of the Lutheran reformers led him to develop a devastating critique of the church in which he had been nurtured. From the lowliest curate, to the most lordly bishop, cardinal or pope, every rank of the clergy was held up to the light of the scriptures, and found wanting. What was needed, in Tyndale's view, was *preachers* who would fearlessly declare the Gospel of Christ.

CHAPTER 1

# TYNDALE'S ORIGINS

## "Upon the borders of Wales"

In one of the earliest accounts of William Tyndale's life, he is said to have been born "upon the borders of Wales". This was the phrase used in the chronicle of Edward Halle, published in 1548. The same words were copied by the martyrologist, John Foxe, in the 1563 edition of his *Actes and Monuments*. His earlier Latin edition of 1559 had "*near* the borders of Wales" (*prope Vualiae fines*). Foxe later modified his wording very slightly, to read "*about* the borders of Wales", and in another place he wrote that it was "on the *edge* of Wales".[1]

Unfortunately these vague descriptions could allow of the possibility that Tyndale was born in any of four English counties (Cheshire, Shropshire, Herefordshire, Gloucestershire). It might even have been thought possible that he was born over the border, in Wales itself.[2]

Over the years, popular opinion has tended to focus upon Gloucestershire as being the region where Tyndale was most likely to have been born. One reason for this is that he is recorded as having lived in the county for a while, in the early 1520s, when he was employed in the household of Sir John Walsh at the manor of Little Sodbury. However, this is a far from adequate reason for claiming Gloucestershire as his county of origin. There is no necessary link between a person's place of birth and his adult place of employment.

## Tyndale-Hychyns

A more plausible reason for assigning Tyndale's birthplace to Gloucestershire is the fact that a number of families were living there who bore the double name of Tyndale and *Hutchins*. It is well known that William Tyndale often used the name of *Hychyns* or *Hutchins*, as found, for example, in his *Parable of the Wicked Mammon*, and *The Obedience of a Christian Man*, both printed in 1528. During the 16th century, and earlier, families with this double name were living in the district of Stinchcombe, North Nibley and Slimbridge.

It has therefore become widely accepted that Tyndale was born in or near one of these Gloucestershire villages, situated in the vale of Berkeley on the east side of the river Severn.[3] A lofty monument was even erected to Tyndale on Nibley Knoll, to commemorate his supposed connection with that locality.

One problem with this theory is that there is no direct evidence to link William Tyndale with any of the various individuals who have been found to possess that name among the contemporary local records. There are at least two other William Tyndales from that area, one of whom died in 1523-4, while the other was still alive in 1542, but these dates prevent any identification with Tyndale the translator, who was martyred in 1536.[4]

## Edward Tyndale

A more promising piece of evidence seemed to be provided by a letter to Cromwell in 1533 from John Stokesley, the bishop of London.[5] In a phrase which he added between the lines, Stokesley mentioned that Edward Tyndale, who was receiver for the lordship of Berkeley, was "brother to Tendall the arch heretic". This position had been held by Edward Tyndale since 1519.[6] He also had a lease of Hurst manor, near Slimbridge.[7] From this information, some have been led to conclude that this is where William Tyndale must have been born. This particular line of argument is unconvincing. For one thing, Stokesley's assertion of Edward's relationship to William may have been no more than a guess, motivated by malice towards Edward Tyndale.[8] Further, even if Edward was the brother of William, his residing at Hurst in the 1520s is no proof that either he or William was born there twenty or thirty years previously. In fact, Edward Tyndale received his lease of Hurst manor in 1516, by a royal grant which described him as being from Tewkesbury.[9] Stokesley's letter therefore does not in any way support the theory that William Tyndale was born in the district of Berkeley.

## A geographical problem

Another problem with locating Tyndale's birthplace in the vale of Berkeley is that it does not entirely merit the description as being "upon the borders of Wales". Although Stinchcombe and the other nearby villages are not much more than ten miles from the Welsh border, this part of Gloucestershire lies to the east of the river Severn and so does not truly border on Wales at any point. If Tyndale was born in Gloucestershire at all, which is not certain, it might have been thought more likely that he would have been born in that portion of the county which lies on the west of the Severn, and which shares a border with Wales for a distance of some twelve miles along the eastern edge of Monmouthshire.

To assist in resolving this question of Tyndale's origins, there is another source of evidence, found in the records of his ordination, to which we will now turn.

CHAPTER 2

# TYNDALE'S ORDINATION

### Subdeacon in the diocese of Hereford

In the biography of Tyndale by J. F. Mozley, published in 1937, attention is drawn to an entry in one of the bishops' registers for the diocese of Hereford, recording that a certain William Hychyns from that diocese was ordained as subdeacon on 10 June 1514. The place of ordination was at the parish church of Whitborne, in Herefordshire, and he was ordained to a "title" of the priory of St. Mary Overie, Southwark.

On the same day, a John Hychyns, from the same diocese, was ordained as acolyte. Two days later, on 12 June, William Hychyns was granted "letters dimissory", enabling him to be ordained to the higher sacred orders outside his home diocese. In view of Tyndale's frequent use of the *alias* "Hutchins", Mozley asks, "Can this be Tyndale and his brother? The date fits, and the family may have dwelt over the Herefordshire border".[10]

A summary of these entries in the register of bishop Richard Mayew had already been published by A. T. Bannister in 1919, though without any mention of a possible connection with Tyndale.[11] A fresh transcript of the Latin text of the register, with abbreviations given in expanded form, and with an English translation appended, is as follows:

## Hereford, County Record Office, MS AL 19/12

(1) [f. 130v] "Ordines sacri et speciales celebrati per reuerendum in Christo patrem et dominum, dominum Ricardum, permissione diuina Herefordensem episcopum, in ecclesia parochiali de Whitborn decimo die mensis Junii anno domini retroscripto [1514] et consecrationis dicti reuerendi patris anno decimo: . . .

*Acoliti seculares:* . . . Johannes Hychyns, Herefordensis diocesis; . . . *Subdiaconi seculares:* . . . Willelmus Hychyns, Herefordensis diocesis, ad titulum prioratus beate Marie de Overey in Sowthwerke, Wintoniensis diocesis."

> "Sacred and special orders conferred by the reverend father and lord in Christ, lord Richard, by divine permission the bishop of Hereford, in the parish church of Whitborne on the 10th day of the month of June, in the year of the Lord as previously written [1514], and in the 10th year of the consecration of the said reverend father: . . .
>
> *Secular acolytes:* . . . John Hychyns, of Hereford diocese; . . . *Secular subdeacons:* . . . William Hychyns, of Hereford diocese, to a title of the priory of the blessed Mary Overie in Southwark, in the diocese of Winchester."

(2) [f. 89v] "Duodecimo die mensis Junii anno domini et loco retroscriptis [1514] concesse sunt per dominum litere dimissorie Willelmo Hychyns subdiacono, quod ad reliquos sacros ordines a quocunque episcopo catholico, sedis apostolice gratiam et sui officii executionem obtinente, licite promoueri possit, non obstante quod in diocese Herefordensi oriundus existit, concurrentibus tum in eo aliis statutis a iure."

> "On the 12th day of the month of June in the year of our Lord and place as previously written [1514], letters dimissory were granted by his lordship to William Hychyns, subdeacon, that it may be permissible for him to be promoted to the remaining sacred orders by any catholic bishop who has obtained grace from the apostolic see and the authority to perform the duties of his office, notwithstanding that he [Hychyns] originates from the diocese of Hereford, there being also other statutes which concur in this as a lawful procedure."

Mozley's reference to this material was given in a footnote that was added to his text at a late stage, "at the eleventh hour", apparently while the book was in course of publication, too late to modify his other references to Tyndale's origins. If Tyndale was a resident of Gloucestershire, which at that time mostly lay within the diocese of Worcester, it might have been expected that he should be ordained under the auspices of the bishop of Worcester rather than the bishop of Hereford. Surprisingly, the significance of this ordination record, as evidence of where Tyndale had spent his early years, has been ignored by later biographers.[12]

## Tyndale's ordination as deacon and priest

Earlier efforts to unearth the details of Tyndale's ordination to the priesthood had not met with success. From the register of bishop Warham, for example, it was discovered that a William Tindale from the diocese of Carlisle was ordained priest in London on 11 March 1503.[13] If this were the future Bible translator, though, it would carry the unlikely implication that he was born before 1480, and would contradict the other evidence that he came from near the Welsh border.

He has also been identified with a Greenwich Observant friar named William Tyndale, who took his monastic vows in 1508, as recorded by an inscription in a printed book belonging to the library of St. Paul's cathedral.[14] This suggested identification similarly lacks plausibility, as none of the accounts of Tyndale the translator make any mention of his being a former monk or friar.

Demaus, in his classic biography of Tyndale, dismissed these suggestions and thought it more probable that he was ordained within the diocese of Lincoln, which at that period covered the city of Oxford where Tyndale spent several years as a student.[15] However, various attempts to locate him in the ordination records of Lincoln, as well as those of Winchester, Ely and Worcester, have been fruitless.[16]

It is now possible to supply the missing details of this aspect of Tyndale's career. The same William

Hychyns who was ordained subdeacon in the diocese of Hereford is found to have been ordained to the higher orders of deacon and priest in the diocese of *London* in 1515.[17] This information is recorded in the register of the bishop of London, Richard Fitzjames. The full entries, accompanied by an English translation, read as follows:

---

London, Guildhall Library, MS 9531/9:

---

(1) [f. 180r] "Die sabbati qua cantatur in ecclesia dei officium misse *Sicientes*, viz. vicesimo quarto die mensis Marcii anno domini millesimo quingentesimo quartodecimo. In ecclesia cathedrali Sancti Pauli, London, venerabilis in Christo pater dominus Johannes dei gratia Calipolensis episcopus, vice et auctoritate dicti reuerendi patris, ordines subscriptos celebrauit generales: . . . *Diaconi:* [f. 180v] . . . Willelmus Hichyns in artibus bacallarius Herfordensis diocesis per literas dimissorias, ad titulum prioratus beate Marie Overey in Suthwerk."

> "On the Saturday on which the office of the Mass known as *Sicientes* is sung in God's church, that is the 24th day of the month of March, A.D. 1514 [= 1515 by modern reckoning of the calendar], in the cathedral church of St. Paul's, London, the venerable father in Christ, lord John [= John Young, suffragan bishop], by the grace of God being bishop of Gallipoli, and in the place

> of and by the authority of the said reverend father [= Fitzjames, bishop of London], conferred the following general orders:. . . *Deacons:* . . . William Hichyns, bachelor of arts, of the diocese of Hereford, by letters dimissory, to a title of the priory of the blessed Mary Overie in Southwark."

(2) [f. 180v] "Sabbato sancto in vigilia pasche, septimo viz. die mensis Aprilis anno domini millesimo quingentesimo decimoquinto. In ecclesia hospitalis Sancti Thome martyris de Acon, ciuitatis London, venerabilis in Christo pater dominus Johannes dei gratia Calipolensis episcopus, vice et auctoritate dicti reuerendi patris, ordines subscriptos celebrauit generales: . . . *Presbiteri:* . . . Willelmus Hychyns in artibus bacallarius Herfordensis [f. 181r] diocesis per literas dimissorias, ad titulum prioratus beate Marie Overey in Suthweke Wintoniensis diocesis."

> "On Holy Saturday, on the eve of Easter, that is the 7th day of the month of April, A.D. 1515, in the church of the hospital of St. Thomas Acon the martyr, in the city of London, the venerable father in Christ, lord John [John Young was master of this hospital, as well as suffragan bishop], by the grace of God being bishop of Gallipoli, and in the place of and by the authority of the said reverend father [Fitzjames], conferred the following general orders: . . . *Priests:* . . . William Hychyns, bachelor of arts, of the diocese of Hereford, by letters dimissory, to a title of the priory of the blessed Mary Overie in Southwark in the diocese of Winchester."

## William Hychyns, B.A. and William Tyndale

The identity of the William Hychyns who was ordained subdeacon in Herefordshire with the William Hychyns who was ordained deacon and priest in London is beyond all doubt. They share the same name, they are both in possession of letters dimissory from Hereford, the chronological sequence is consistent, and on each occasion they are ordained to a "title" belonging to the Augustinian priory of St. Mary Overie at Southwark (now Southwark cathedral). Allocation of such a "title" was a normal means of providing financial support for newly ordained members of the secular clergy, until such time as they might be given a benefice.

This mention of Hychyns' degree of bachelor of arts, not recorded in the Hereford register, is significant as it links him with the William Hychyns who was at that time studying at Oxford University. The university registers show that William Hychyns graduated B.A. on 4 July 1512, and M.A. on 2 July 1515,[18] which is strictly consistent with the degree attributed to the Hychyns who was ordained to the diaconate and priesthood in March-April 1515. That Tyndale became a master of arts was acknowledged by Thomas More.[19] Since the records of the university do not contain any reference to another William Hychyns or Tyndale during this period, it is virtually certain that these entries all relate to one individual, William Tyndale *alias* Hychyns or Hutchins, the future Bible translator.

In view of Tyndale's later criticisms of the clergy, it is most interesting to see how his earlier career in many respects conformed with the traditional ecclesiastical pattern, quietly treading the well worn path of ordination as subdeacon, deacon, and priest. Over the next few years he would undergo a revolution in his thinking, which would lead him to condemn such ceremonies as little more than an empty charade. He was to call the titles of subdeacon and deacon "vain names without office". What made a true priest, he would say, was not the ceremony of ordination, but the command of Christ in sending out his disciples to preach.[20]

### Tyndale and Colet

The record of Tyndale's ordination to the diaconate and priesthood in 1515 also provides the earliest evidence of his visiting London. As it was only a few days journey from Oxford, it would not be surprising to find that he went up to London from time to time, but there is no other evidence that he did so before 1523, when he approached Cuthbert Tunstall for support for his Bible translation project.

The reason why he chose to be ordained in London rather than in the diocese of Lincoln, in which Oxford then lay, is not certain. It may have been simply a matter of convenience, so that he could be ordained successively as deacon and priest in the same town and with a single journey: since only a fortnight separated the two ceremonies, Tyndale was probably able to stay in London in the interval. To attend two successive ordination services in the Lincoln diocese at this time would have required him to travel a much greater distance, for these were scheduled to take place at Dunstable on 3 March, Peterborough on 24 March, and in Lincoln cathedral on 7 April.[21]

Tyndale may also have had other motives for visiting the capital. The current dean of St. Paul's was none other than John Colet, a noted critic of ecclesiastical abuses. At this period, Colet was engaged in a bitter struggle with his bishop, Richard Fitzjames, who charged him with heresy.[22] It is not unlikely that Colet would have been present at Tyndale's ordination as deacon, which took place at St. Paul's. Whether or not they became personally acquainted is unknown, but it is reasonable to suppose that Tyndale was aware of Colet's emphasis on the need for certain reforms. While in London he may have found the opportunity to hear Colet preach. He could also have previously read a copy of Colet's 1512 sermon to Convocation, in which he had rebuked the clergy for their inveterate worldliness and had even ventured to criticise the bishops, in passages such as:

> "Prelates are chosen oftentimes more by favour of men than by the grace of God. Therefore truly have we not a few times bishops full little spiritual, men rather worldly than heavenly, savouring more the spirit of this world than the spirit of Christ."[23]

Tyndale's later remarks on the shortcomings of priests and prelates contain many echoes of the kind of criticisms that Colet had made. In doctrinal matters Colet was not a reformer. Tyndale's doctrinal views were shaped far more by the influence of Luther than by anything which Colet had said. It has also been plausibly suggested that Tyndale was influenced by the Lollard tradition of religious dissent, which went back to the time of John Wyclif in the 14th century. Far more allowance should further be made for the extent to which his beliefs were based on his own independent study of the scriptures. However, Colet's well publicised remarks on the need for reform of the clergy can hardly have failed to have an impact on Tyndale's thinking.

An event which was arousing a degree of anti-clerical sentiment in London at this time was the murder of Richard Hunne, which had taken place in December 1514.[24] Hunne was in prison, largely as a result of his opposition to the greed and arrogance of the clergy. When his body was found hanging in his cell one morning, it was pretended that he had committed suicide, but there was evidence that he had first been murdered. One of those implicated in this crime was Dr. Horsey, the chancellor of the bishop of London. Horsey was energetically protected by his bishop, and finally escaped conviction through the king giving instructions for his acquittal. Since the investigation of Hunne's murder was still in progress during Tyndale's visit to London, the affair would not have escaped his notice, as it gave rise to widespread gossip and rumour. The case may have contributed to his later severity of language in speaking of criminal members of the clergy who had used their status in order to avoid the punishment they deserved.[25]

## Tyndale's birthplace

Now that the early connection of Tyndale with the diocese of Hereford is well established, there is an increased likelihood that he was born either in Herefordshire or in one of the parts of Gloucestershire that used to belong to the Hereford diocese, including that portion of Gloucestershire which borders on Wales, to the west of the river Severn. In the 1522 military survey of Gloucestershire, for example, there were two individuals by the name of William and Richard Heochyns living in this area, at Nass, and another William Heochyns living at Purton nearby.[26] Others by the name of Hutchins, Hychys, and Hychyns appear in the Hereford probate registers as living at Newnham, Lydney and Awre in the 15th century, all in the same part of Gloucestershire.[27]

The existence of several branches of the Hutchins family in this part of the county is therefore well established, and although it has not been ascertained whether any of them also used the alternative name, Tyndale, there is a distinct possibility that William Tyndale *alias* Hychyns was related to them and came from that area. Since, on the other hand, the Hereford diocese did not include the villages of southern Gloucestershire, east of the Severn, the notion that Tyndale was born in the area of Stinchcombe, Slimbridge or Nibley Knoll should probably now be discarded.

It so happens that in the area of Gloucestershire to the west of the Severn, there is evidence of the presence of a number of individuals holding Lollard beliefs, towards the end of the 15th and at the beginning of the 16th century. The registers of the Hereford diocese record the examination of sixteen suspected Lollards from the area of Woolaston, Aylburton, Lydney and

Purton in 1470-2, most of whom were forced to abjure.[28] Their "heretical" views were said to include denial of the traditional doctrines concerning transubstantiation, purgatory, indulgences, confession, and prayers to the saints. Some of them were also guilty of possessing and reading portions of the Bible in the English language: no doubt this was the Wyclif translation. The bishops' attempts to stamp out these dangerous dissidents were not wholly successful. In about 1499 there were two Lollards who were burnt to death as heretics, at the town of Lydney. In 1511 another Lollard, said to be from Woolaston and Micheldean, was examined by bishop Mayew.

If Tyndale's family were living in this district, it is inevitable that he would have become acquainted with the activities and teachings of the local Lollards, and the persecutions which they suffered, and this may well have been one factor which helped to shape his later religious outlook.[29] It would be unrealistic, however, to suppose that he openly adopted Lollard beliefs prior to 1515, as this would have been an obstacle to his ordination as priest.

The relationship of William Tyndale to the John Hychyns who was ordained acolyte at Whitborne, on the same day as his own ordination as subdeacon, is not clear. Tyndale did have a brother named John, but he was a merchant rather than a member of the clergy.[30] It seems more likely that the John Hychyns who was ordained was a more distant relation, perhaps a cousin. The Hereford bishops' registers record that a John Hychyns, possibly the same person, was ordained as subdeacon on 11 April 1517, and deacon on 6 June

1517, to a "title" of the hospital of St. John the Baptist at Ludlow.[31]

### Estimates of Tyndale's date of birth

In George Offor's account of Tyndale's life, published in 1836, it was estimated that he was born "about the year 1477". From the mid-19th century onwards there was a revised consensus that the year of Tyndale's birth was 1484. This was the view of Anderson, Walter and Demaus.[32] When fresh information came to light regarding the dates when Tyndale obtained his degrees at Oxford university, a new date was proposed for his birth. In his 1886 revision of Demaus' biography, R. Lovett fixed the year of Tyndale's birth as being "about 1495".[33] Those who had already commemorated Tyndale's four hundredth anniversary in 1884 now had a second opportunity to celebrate in 1895. A few years later, the *Dictionary of National Biography* more cautiously assigned a date of 1490-95, which has continued to be regarded as authoritative.

The next attempt at greater precision came in 1937, when Mozley's new biography of Tyndale amended his date of birth to 1494.[34] Twelve years later, Mozley was reported as preferring a date of 1491 or 1492.[35] However, his previous pronouncement won general acceptance, and the hypothetical birth date of 1494 has been widely treated as an established fact. On this basis 1994 was selected as the year for the Tyndale quincentenary celebrations.

The time has come to make another adjustment, to take account of the new information regarding the date of Tyndale's ordination to the priesthood. Under canon law a person could not normally be ordained as priest before reaching the age of twenty-four. Reckoning backwards from the known date of Tyndale's ordination, this would imply that he was born no later than 7 April 1491. This in turn would mean that he was at least twenty-one at the time of receiving his B.A. degree. Although it was possible to be ordained several years earlier than the required canonical age, by purchasing a papal dispensation, no documentary evidence has been produced to show that he did so.

CHAPTER 3

# TYNDALE AT OXFORD

In this chapter we will consider the information which can be derived from the university registers concerning Tyndale's years at Oxford. The intellectual content of his arts course, the books which he may have studied, and the contemporary ethos of university life, have been covered in considerable detail by others who have written on the subject, and will not be repeated here.[36]

It has already been mentioned that Tyndale received his B.A. degree in 1512 and his M.A. in 1515. On the incorrect assumption that his B.A. course lasted four years and that an M.A. could not be obtained in under seven years, some of Tyndale's more recent biographers have concluded that he therefore began his undergraduate studies at Oxford in 1508.[37] However, from the university archives it is evident that he completed his B.A. in a much shorter time, in just two years and a term, as was correctly reported by C. W. Boase and R. Lovett in 1885-6.[38] This would mean that he started his university career no earlier than 1510, when he was probably at least eighteen years of age, and that he became master of arts in about five and a half years. The short length of his course may reflect his exceptional diligence as a student.

In the university's *Register of Congregation*, there are no less than nine entries relating to William

Hychyns (that is, Tyndale), of which only the first five appear to have been previously published. The original entries, together with an English translation, read as follows:

---

Oxford University Archives, NEP/*supra*/Register G
"Register of Congregation 1505-17"

---

(1) [f. 145v: 13 May 1512] "Hychyns: Eodem die supplicat Willelmus Hychyns, scolaris artium, quatenus studium duorum [i.e. duorum annorum] cum termino infra vniuersitatem, cum responsione vni bachallario in Quadragesima, cum creatione vnius generalis et duabus variationibus in parviso, et oppositione et responsione ratione officii collectoris in parviso, sufficiat. Hec est concessa quod [i.e. sic quod] determinet proxima Quadragesima et bis disputet preter formam."

> "Hychyns: On the same day, William Hychyns, scholar in arts, supplicates that the study of two years and a term within the university, with a responsion to one bachelor in Lent, with the 'creation of one general' and two 'variations' *in Parviso*, and an opposition and responsion *in Parviso*, under the Collector, may suffice. This grace was granted on condition that he 'determines' during the next Lent and disputes twice beyond what is formally required."

In case the translation might appear only slightly less unintelligible than the Latin, a brief explanation of these procedures will be appropriate.[39] To obtain the degree of bachelor of arts, a student had to take part in a series of oral disputations, held at intervals during his university course. In such disputations the person who proposed the subject of debate was known as the opponent, and the one who answered him was the respondent. The student had to take the part of opponent and respondent on different occasions, described respectively as an opposition and a responsion. "Variations" are said to be a form of disputation in which the same person presents the arguments both for and against a set proposition. The disputation known as a "creation general" (*creatio generalis*) marked a student's transition to the second stage of his course, entitling him to be called a "sophister general" (*sophista generalis*). Most of these formal exercises took place in the university buildings known as the "new schools", though they were formerly held in the porch of St. Mary's church (*in parviso*). The graduate who supervised the disputations was known as the "collector".

The responsion to a bachelor in the season of Lent was a disputation between an undergraduate and a newly graduated B.A. On such occasions the bachelor of arts was said to "determine", that is to preside over the disputation, acting as opponent, while an undergraduate would act as respondent. "Determining" was a standard requirement which nearly all new bachelors of arts had to fulfil during the Lent which next followed after their graduation. When Tyndale "determined" in the Lent which followed his admission as B.A., he was required to take part in two additional disputations, as a modest compensation for the shortness of his B.A. course.

* * *

(2) [f. 150(a)v: 4 July 1512] "Admissi in artibus: Eodem die supplicat [*sic*: "sup"] admissus est ad lecturam alicuius libri decretalium [*sic*] . . . dominus Willelmus Hychyns."

> "Admitted in arts: On the same day, . . . sir William Hychyns . . . supplicates/is admitted to the reading of a book of decretals."

This entry was recorded in a negligent fashion. The word *supplicat*, abbreviated as *sup*, was the normal way of commencing a request for a dispensation, but this was clearly inappropriate in a passage recording the admission of a number of students as bachelors of arts, and this word should have been deleted. Worse still, the admission of bachelors of arts to "reading a book of decretals" was an impossibility, as such a book was suitable only for a student of law, and the new bachelors of law are listed in another entry. The entry relating to Hychyns, or Tyndale, should have finished as "book of the faculty of arts". Bachelors of arts were expected to lecture on one of the standard texts of the arts course, for the benefit of undergraduate students. To be admitted to the "reading" of such a book was the equivalent of being awarded the B.A. degree.

* * *

(3) [f. 165v: February 1513] "Sequuntur nomina determinatorum . . . dominus Willelmus Huchens."

> "The names of those who "determined" are as follows: . . . sir William Huchens."

As previously described, the formal disputations known as "determining" were required of bachelors of arts in their first year after graduation, and took place each Lent.

* * *

(4) [f. 246r: 26 June 1515] "Eodem die licentiati sunt in artibus dominus Willelmus Hychyns, dominus Robartus Squere et dominus Ioannes Stevynson."

> "On the same day sir William Hychyns, sir Robert Squere, and sir John Stevynson, were licensed in arts."

* * *

(5) [f. 260v: 2 July 1515] Eodem die creati sunt in artibus magistri quorum nomina sequuntur, videlicet . . . magister Willelmus Hochyns."

> "On the same day those whose names follow were created masters of arts, viz. . . . master William Hochyns."

* * *

(6) [f. 274v: 13 December 1515] "Presentes: Eodem die supplicant omnes presentes quatenus gratiose cum eis dispensetur pro sua necessaria regentia. Hec est concessa simpliciter; presentibus Shelley, Squere, Hychyns."

> "Present: On the same day all those present supplicate that they may freely be dispensed from their "necessary regency". This grace was granted unconditionally, Shelley, Squere and Hychyns being present."

New masters of arts were theoretically required to serve as "regents" for their first two years, an obligation which was known as "necessary regency". The regents were responsible for giving lectures and supervising the disputations and the general administration of the university. In practice they could be dispensed from their "necessary regency", if there were a sufficient number of other masters of arts available to carry out the routine duties. Hence Tyndale was able to obtain release from these duties after only a few months.

* * *

(7) [f. 276v: 1 February 1516] "Presentes: Eodem die supplicant omnes magistri presentes quatenus quilibet eorum possint dare votum, petere et pronuntiare gratias in congregatione in habitu non regentie. Hec est concessa simpliciter, presentibus Appulby, Hycchyns, Blunstone, Falowfylde, <Cornyshe.>"

> "Present: On the same day all masters present supplicate that any of them may give their vote, and seek and pronounce graces in congregation, without being dressed as regents. This grace was granted unconditionally, Appulby, Hycchyns, Blunstone, Falowfylde and Cornyshe being present."

* * *

(8) [f.279r: 8 March 1516] “Presentes: Eodem die supplicant omnes presentes quatenus dispensetur cum eis gratiose vt non teneantur ad generales processiones nec conuocationes, non obstante quocunque statuto in oppositum, sic quod magister Pantrey sit particeps. Hec est concessa simpliciter; <presentibus magistris Hychyns etc.>”

> “Present: On the same day all those present supplicate that they may freely be dispensed from being obliged to take part in general processions and convocations, notwithstanding any statute to the contrary, on condition that master Pantrey would participate. This grace was granted without further condition, master Hychyns etc. being present.”

In this entry and the following, the name of Hychyns seems to be in a different ink, but the script is contemporary and there is no reason to suspect an unauthorised insertion.

* * *

(9) [same page and date] “Eodem die supplicant omnes presentes quatenus non teneantur ad exequias nec missas nec depositiones. Hec est concessa simpliciter; <presentibus Hychyns.>”

> “On the same day all those present supplicate that they should not be obliged to attend services for the dead, or masses, or “depositions”. This grace was granted unconditionally, Hychyns [and others] being present.”

“Depositions” were the giving of testimony regarding the suitability of candidates for university degrees.

* * *

There can be no doubt that all these items refer to the same William Hychyns. Although only his surname is given in the last four entries, there was no other recent master of arts who had this name. Further, in the 6th and 7th entries, the other accompanying names all relate to masters of arts who had received their degree on the same day as Hychyns. It may also be noticed, incidentally, that whereas most of his contemporaries were given a range of minor official responsibilities within the university, his name does not appear to be included in the various lists of such officers.

The impression given by this series of dispensations is that Hychyns, or rather Tyndale, did his utmost to avoid participation in the ceremonial duties normally performed by a master of arts. The final dispensation might even be construed as reflecting a changed attitude towards the Roman Catholic doctrine of the mass. However, a scholar might have had other reasons for wishing to be exempted from ceremonial obligations, whether on the grounds of expense or because of other demands on his time, and it would be unwise to read too much into Tyndale’s “graces”. His reformed doctrinal views may not have begun to take definite shape until some years later, after reading the works of Martin Luther.

## Was Tyndale still a "child" when he went to Oxford?

As has been seen, Tyndale began his university studies in 1510, when he was probably aged at least eighteen. This raises a problem, as the account by John Foxe says that he was "brought up from a child in the university of Oxford", where he resided at Magdalen Hall.[40] This has been taken to mean that Tyndale was still a schoolboy for his first few years at Oxford, attending Magdalen College School, and that he did not immediately begin a course of study in the university itself.[41]

On the basis of two dubious assumptions, firstly that he was not born until 1494, and secondly that his university course began in 1508, it has been supposed that he began attending Magdalen Hall and the adjacent school in 1506 at the age of "twelve".[42] If, however, his twelfth birthday was no later than 1503 and his arts course did not begin until 1510, did Tyndale therefore spend over six years at Magdalen Hall before enrolling as a university student?

In fact, in the only reference which Foxe makes to Magdalen Hall, Tyndale is described as living there while he instructed certain fellows and students of Magdalen College in the knowledge of the scriptures: this is not the activity of a schoolboy, but a graduate. It is hence quite possible that he had studied for his first degree at one of the other colleges.

There are grounds for thinking that Foxe's phrase, "brought up from a child", was not based on any fresh evidence which had come to his hands. In Halle's chronicle of 1548, it is stated that Tyndale was "brought up in the university of Oxford", without adding that he was still a child. Then in John Bale's *Illustrium Maioris Britanniae Scriptorum. . . Summarium*, printed in the same year, there is a reference to Tyndale as "applying himself to studies at Oxford from the time of his youth" (*Oxonii ab adolescente studiis incumbens*).[43]

It looks as if Foxe may have interpreted Halle and Bale as meaning that Tyndale was no more than a "child", whereas their use of the expressions "brought up" and "adolescent" could have been intended to apply to a young adult. If so, then Tyndale may have begun his university studies in 1510 as soon as he arrived in Oxford, without any preceding period of school education there, in which case he may have received his earlier education at a local grammar school somewhere in the diocese of Hereford.

Although there was some justification for Mozley's claim that "Foxe's account of Tyndale has been triumphantly vindicated by modern discoveries",[44] it will by no means be thought that Foxe was incapable of error. An egregious example of a Foxian lapse can be found in his assertion, in another part of his work, that Tyndale was among the first members of Cardinal College in Oxford.[45] Since that college was only begun in 1525, at a time when Tyndale was out of the country and occupied in publishing the first edition of his translation of the New Testament, the inclusion of Tyndale as a member of the college was manifestly incorrect.

In the same way Foxe may have been mistaken as to Tyndale's age when he became an Oxford student.

It still remains possible that Tyndale received part of his education at Magdalen College School before 1510, but it would be unsafe to rely on Foxe's account as providing sufficient proof of this.

CHAPTER 4

# EARLY NARRATIVES OF TYNDALE'S LIFE

## (a) Edward Halle

*The Vnion of the two noble and illustrate famelies of Lancastre and Yorke* (1548)

[f. 227r: under the year 1535] "This year in the month of September, William Tyndale otherwise called Hichyns was by the cruelty of the clergy of Louvain condemned and burned in a town beside Brussels in Brabant, called Vilvorde [in fact, arrested in May 1535 and burned in October 1536]. This man translated the New Testament into English and first put it in print, and likewise he translated the five books of Moses, Joshua, Judges, Ruth, the books of the Kings and the books of Paralipomenon [= Chronicles], Nehemiah or the first book of Esdras,[46] the prophet Jonah, and no more of ye holy scripture. He made also diverse treatises, which of many were well liked and highly praised, and of many utterly despised and abhorred, and especially of the most part of the bishops of this realm, who often by their great labours caused proclamations to be made against his books, and got them condemned and burnt, as well the New Testament as other works of his doings.

Such as best knew him reported him to be a very sober man, born upon the borders of Wales, and brought up in the university of Oxford, and in life and conversation unreprovable. And at the last, being in Oxford, Luther then setting forth certain works against the bishop of Rome, Tyndale, occasioned by them to search the scriptures whether Luther said the truth or no, did thereby not only himself attain the knowledge of the usurped authority of the bishop of Rome, and his superstitious and damnable doctrines that he had taught and published through all christendom, but also lamenting the ignorant state that his native country of England was in, who altogether were wrapped in errors, thought it his duty, for that God had revealed the light of his Gospel to him, to bestow his talent to the honour of God and profit of his country, and thought no way so good to reduce the people from their error as first to make them acquainted with God's word, that they might know what God's will was that we should do, and what the bishop of Rome said that we must do. And therefore first, as is aforesaid, he translated into English the New Testament, a work no doubt very notable and to him very painful, for that he was forced to flee his own native country, and to live in a strange land among people that as well varied from his manners as the persons were to him unknown.

Amongst whom after great pains by him taken, and many and diverse treatises by him published, he was at Antwerp this year [f. 227v] by one Phillips, an Englishman and then a scholar at Louvain, betrayed and taken, and as many said, not without the help and procurement of some bishops of this realm. But true it is, that after he had been in prison more than a year and almost forgotten, he was laboured for by letters written by the lord Cromwell, and then in all haste because he would recant no part of his doings, was burned as you have heard before. But yet this report did the procurator general there (which we call here the lieutenant) make of him, that he was *homo doctus, pius et bonus*, that is to say, learned, godly, and good."

* * *

### (b) John Bale

*Illustrium Maioris Britanniae Scriptorum. . . Summarium* ("Ipswich" [Wesel], 31 July 1548)

— with variants of the 1557 edition (printed in Basle) —

[f. 220v] "Guilhelmus Tyndale, seu Hychyns, *Anglus [1557 omits], ad multorum in Christo salutem natus, Oxonii ab adolescente studiis incumbens, bonas literas abunde hausit, Graece ac Latine peritus. Grandescens paulatim nouellus hic Iesu Christi Apostolus, eruditione, fide, ac uitae innocentia clarus, in *hac regione post Ioannem Wicleuum primus habebatur, qui eius fortiter promouerit causam aduersus Balaamitas [Anglica regione primus habebatur, post Ioannem Vuicleuum, qui diuinae ueritatis contra iniquos Balaamitas promoueret causam 1557], ac populum recta in [erga 1557] Deum fide instituerit [-eret 1557]. Paratus profecto semper erat [+ vir pius 1557] , nihil non strennue [strenue 1557] in ea tam pia obire functione. Nemo ueterum scriptorum lympidius Christum docuit, nemo [+ pessimorum 1557] Antichristorum fallacias apertius detegit [detexit 1557] . . ."

> "William Tyndale or Hychyns, *an Englishman [1557 omits], was born for the salvation of

many in Christ. Applying himself to studies at Oxford from the time of his youth, he drank deeply of good literature, becoming skilled in Greek and Latin. This new Apostle of Jesus Christ, gradually increasing in scholarship and in faith, and well known for his uprightness of life, was held to be the first man in *this country [the country of England 1557] since John Wyclif to carry forward with vigour *Wyclif's cause [the cause of divine truth 1557] against the [+ wicked 1557] Balaamites, and to instruct the people in true faith in God. He [+ the devout man 1557] was indeed always ready to undertake with great energy anything that would help to achieve this most holy purpose. None of the old writers taught more clearly concerning Christ, no one revealed more openly the false teachings of the [+ most evil 1557] Antichrists. . ."

* * *

### (c) John Foxe

Foxe printed a detailed account of Tyndale's life, of which he gave several different versions. Reprinted below are just those portions of his narrative which relate to Tyndale's earlier years, up to and including his time at Oxford.

*Actes and Monuments* (1563)

[p. 520] "This good man William Tyndall, the faithful minister and constant martyr of Christ, was born upon ye borders of Wales, and brought up even of a child in the university of Oxford, being always of most upright manners and pure life."

*Actes and Monuments* (1570)

[p. 1224] "William Tyndall, the faithful minister and constant martyr of Christ, was born about the borders of Wales, and brought up from a child in the university of Oxford, where he by long continuance grew up and increased as well in the knowledge of tongues and other liberal arts, as especially in the knowledge of the scriptures, whereunto his mind was singularly addicted: insomuch that he, lying then in Magdalen Hall, read privily to certain students and fellows of Magdalen College some parcel of divinity, instructing them in the knowledge and truth of the scriptures. Whose manners also and conversation, being correspondent to the same, were such that all they which knew him reputed and esteemed him to be a man of most virtuous disposition, and of life unspotted. Thus he, in the university of Oxford increasing more and more in learning, and proceeding in degrees of the schools, spying his time, removed from thence to the university of Cambridge."

*The Whole Workes of W. Tyndall, Iohn Frith, and Doct. Barnes* (1572-3)

[sig. A.iii.r] "First touching the birth and parentage of this blessed martyr in Christ, he was born in the edge of Wales. . ."

[etc. as in 1570, with only minor variations].

CHAPTER 5

# TYNDALE'S VIEWS ON PRIESTS AND PREACHERS

The purpose of this chapter is to present, in chronological order, those portions of Tyndale's writings which contain his thoughts on the subject of Christian priesthood, and the responsibilities of the preacher, together with his criticisms of a widespread failure of the clergy to preach the Gospel and to instruct the people in biblical teaching.

In connection with the material previously presented on the subject of Tyndale's ordination as a priest within the traditional church, it is interesting to see how he later came to emphasise the concept of the priesthood of every Christian believer. The authority to preach, he affirmed, was conferred by the command of Christ in sending out his disciples, rather than by any ceremony of ordination, and the authority to appoint a preacher or elder lay with each congregation. His views on these and many other topics, including such themes as female ministry and theological education, are included in the following extracts.[47]

The wording of the text is based on the original editions of Tyndale's writings. The spelling, however, has been modernised, generally conforming with the 19th century Parker Society edition, whose page references are inserted in brackets. Subheadings have also been added.

## *The Parable of the Wicked Mammon* (1528)

### The preacher's income

[I. 95] "Among Christian men, love maketh all things common. Every man is other's debtor, and every man is bound to minister to his neighbour, and to supply his neighbour's lack of that wherewith God hath endued him. As thou seest in the world, how the lords and officers minister peace in the commonwealth, punish murderers, thieves and evil doers, and to maintain their order and estate, do the commons minister to them again rent, tribute, toll, and custom: so in the [96] Gospel, the curates which in every parish preach the Gospel ought of duty to receive an honest living for them and their households, and even so ought the other officers which are necessarily required in the commonwealth of Christ. We need not to use filthy lucre in the Gospel, to chop and change and to play the taverners, altering the word of God, as they do their wines to their most advantage, and to fashion God's word after every man's mouth, or to abuse the name of Christ to obtain thereby authority and power to feed our slow bellies."

### The preacher's reward

[100] "Of this apostle, hark what Paul saith (in the [first] to the Corinthians ix): 'If I preach,' saith he, 'I have nought to rejoice in, for necessity is put unto me',

as who should say, God hath made me so. 'Woe is unto me if I preach not. If I do it willingly,' saith he, 'then have I my reward,' that is, then am I sure that God's Spirit is in me, and that I am elect to eternal life. 'If I do it against my will, an office [101] is committed unto me,' that is, if I do it not of love to God, but to get a living thereby, and for a worldly purpose, and had lever [= rather] otherwise live, then I do that office which God hath put me in, and yet please not God myself.

Note now, if this apostle preach not, as many do not, which not only make themselves apostles but also compel men to take them for greater than apostles, yea, for greater than Christ himself, then woe is unto him, that is, his damnation is just. If he preach and his heart not right, yet ministereth he the office that God hath put him in, and they that have the Spirit of God hear the voice of God, yea, though he speak in an ass. Moreover, howsoever he preacheth, he hath not to rejoice in that he preacheth. But and if he preach willingly, with a true heart, and of conscience to God, then hath he his reward, that is, then feeleth he the earnest of eternal life, and the working of the Spirit of God in him. And as he feeleth God's goodness and mercy, so be thou sure he feeleth his own infirmity, weakness, and unworthiness, and mourneth and [ac]knowledgeth his sin, in that the heart will not arise to work with that full lust and love that is in Christ our Lord, and nevertheless is yet at peace with God, through faith and trust in Christ Jesu. For the earnest of the Spirit that worketh in him testifieth and beareth witness unto his heart that God hath chosen him, and that his grace shall suffice him, which grace is now not idle in him. In his works putteth he no trust. . ."

[102] "Now if thou compare deed to deed, there is difference betwixt washing of dishes and preaching of the word of God; but as touching to please God, none at all: for neither that nor this pleaseth, but as far forth as God hath chosen a man, hath put his Spirit in him, and purified his heart by faith and trust in Christ."

---

*The Obedience of a Christian Man* (1528)

---

### Knowledge of the scriptures

[I. 146] "They will say haply, 'The scripture requireth a pure mind and a quiet mind, and therefore the layman, because he is altogether cumbered with worldly business, cannot understand them.' If that be the cause, then it is a plain case that our prelates understand not the scriptures themselves, for no layman is so tangled with worldly business as they are. The great things of the world are ministered by them, neither do the lay people any great thing but at their assignment.

'If the scripture were in the mother tongue,' they will say, 'then would the lay people understand it every man after his own ways.' Wherefore serveth the curate, but to teach them the right way? Wherefore were the holy days made, but that the people should come and learn? Are ye not abominable schoolmasters, in that ye take so great wages, if ye will not teach? If ye would teach, how could ye do it so well, and with so great profit, as when the lay people have the scripture before them in their mother tongue? For then should they see, by the order of the text, whether thou jugglest or not. And then would they believe it, because it is the scripture of God, though thy living be never so abominable. Where now, because your living and your preaching are so contrary, and because they grope out in every sermon your open and manifest lies, and smell your unsatiable covetousness, they believe you not when you preach truth.

But alas, the curates themselves (for the most part) wot no more what the New or Old Testament meaneth than do the Turks. Neither know they of any more than that they read at mass, matins and evensong, which yet they understand not. Neither care they, but even to mumble up so much every day (as the pie and popinjay speak, they wot not what) to fill their bellies withal. If they will not let the layman have the word of God in his mother tongue, yet let the priests have it, which for a great part of them do understand no Latin at all, but sing, and say, and patter all day, with the lips only, that which the heart understandeth not."

### Absentee clergymen

[147] "When a whole parish of us hire a schoolmaster to teach our children, what reason is it that we should be compelled to pay this schoolmaster his wages, and he should have licence to go where he will, and to dwell in another country, and to leave our children untaught? Doth not the pope so? [148] Have we not given up our tithes of courtesy unto one for to

teach us God's word, and cometh not the pope and compelleth us to pay it violently to them that never teach? Maketh he not one parson which cometh never at us? Yea, one shall have five or six, or as many as he can get, and wotteth oftentimes where never one of them standeth. Another is made vicar, to whom he giveth a dispensation to go where he will, and to set in a parish priest which can but minister a sort of dumb ceremonies. And he, because he hath most labour and least profit, polleth on his part, and setteth here a mass-penny, there a trental, yonder *dirige*-money, and for his bead-roll, with a confession-penny, and such like. And thus are we never taught, and are yet nevertheless compelled, yea, compelled to hire many costly schoolmasters. These deeds are verily against Christ. Shall we therefore judge you by your deeds, as Christ commandeth? So are ye false prophets, and the disciples of Antichrist, or of Against-Christ."

### The need to preach both the law and the gospel

[156] "Howbeit my meaning is that as a master teacheth his apprentice to know all the points of the mete-yard, first how many inches, how many feet, and the half-yard, the quarter, and the nail, and then teacheth him to mete other things thereby, even so will I that ye teach the people God's law, and what obedience God requireth of us unto father and mother, master, lord, king, and all superiors, and with what friendly love he commandeth one to love another. And teach them to know that natural venom and birth-poison, which moveth the very hearts of us to rebel against the ordinances and will of God, and prove that

no man is righteous in the sight of God, but that we are all damned by the law. And then, when thou hast meeked them and feared them with the law, teach them the testament and promises which God hath made unto us in Christ, and how merciful and kind he is, and how much he loveth us in Christ. And teach them the principles and the ground of the faith, and what the sacraments signify, and then shall the Spirit work with thy preaching, and make them feel.

So would it come to pass, that as we know by natural wit what followeth of a true principle of natural reason, even so, by the principles of the faith, and by the plain scriptures, and by the circumstances of the text, should we judge all men's exposition and all men's doctrine, and should receive the best and refuse the worst. I would have you to teach them also the properties and manner of speakings of the scripture, and how to expound proverbs and similitudes. And then, if they go abroad and walk by the fields and meadows of all manner doctors and philosophers, they could catch no harm: they should discern the poison from the honey, and bring home nothing but that which is wholesome.

## The corrupting effects of a theological education

But now do ye clean contrary: ye drive them from God's word, and will let no man come thereto, until he have [157] been two years master of art. First, they nosel [= nurture] them in sophistry, and in *benefundatum*. And there corrupt they their judgments with apparent arguments, and with alleging unto them texts of logic, of natural *philautia*, of metaphysic, and moral philosophy, and of all manner books of Aristotle, and of all manner doctors which they yet never saw. Moreover, one holdeth this, another that; one is a Real, another a Nominal. What wonderful dreams have they of their predicaments, universals, second intentions, [158] *quiddities, haecceities*, and relatives; and whether *species fundata in chimera* be *vera species*; and whether this proposition be true, *Non ens est aliquid*; whether *ens* be *aequivocum*, or *univocum. Ens* is a voice only, say some. *Ens* is *univocum,* saith another, and descendeth into *ens creatum,* and into *ens increatum, per modos intrinsecos.*

When they have thiswise brawled eight, ten, or twelve or more years, and after that their judgments are utterly corrupt, then they begin their divinity, not at the scripture, but every man taketh a sundry doctor, which doctors are as sundry and as diverse, the one contrary unto the other, as there are diverse fashions and monstrous shapes, none like another, among our sects of religion. Every religion, every university, and almost every man, hath a sundry divinity. Now whatsoever opinions every man findeth with his doctor, that is his gospel, and that only is true with him, and that holdeth he all his life long, and every man, to maintain his doctor withal, corrupteth the scripture and fashioneth it after his own imagination, as a potter doth his clay. Of what text thou provest hell, will another prove purgatory; another *limbo patrum*; and another the [159] assumption of our lady; and another shall prove of the same text that an ape hath a tail. And of what text the grey friar proveth that our lady was without original sin, of the same shall the black friar prove that she was conceived in original sin. And all this do they with apparent reasons, [160] with false similitudes and likenesses, and with arguments and persuasions of man's wisdom.

### The idolatry of man's wisdom

Now there is no other division or heresy in the world save man's wisdom, and when man's foolish wisdom interpreteth the scripture. Man's wisdom scattereth, divideth, and maketh sects: while the wisdom of one is that a white coat is best to serve God in, and another saith a black, another a grey, another a blue. And while one saith that God will hear your prayer in this place, another saith in that place. And while one saith this place is holier, and another that place is holier; and this religion is holier than that; and this saint is greater with God than that; and an hundred thousand like things. Man's wisdom is plain idolatry, neither is there any other idolatry than to imagine of God after man's wisdom. God is not man's imagination, but that only which he saith of himself."

### False obedience

[173] "O how sore differeth the doctrine of Christ and his apostles from the doctrine of the pope and of his apostles! For if any man will obey neither father nor mother, neither lord nor master, neither king nor prince, the same needeth but only to take the mark of the beast, that is, to shave himself a monk, a friar, or a priest, and is then immediately free and exempted from all service and obedience due unto man. He that will obey no man (as they will not) is most acceptable unto them. The more disobedient that thou art unto God's

ordinances, the more apt and meet art thou for theirs. Neither is the professing, vowing, and swearing obedience unto their ordinances, any other thing than the defying, denying, and forswearing obedience unto the ordinances of God."

### Begin by preaching against the bishops

[185] "Bishops, they only can minister the temporal sword, their office, the preaching of God's word, laid apart: which they will neither do nor suffer any man to do, but slay with the temporal sword, which they have gotten out of the hand of all princes, them that would. The preaching of God's word is hateful and contrary unto them. Why? For it is impossible to preach Christ, except thou preach against Antichrist, that is [186] to say, them which with their false doctrine and violence of sword enforce to quench the true doctrine of Christ. And as thou canst heal no disease except thou begin at the root, even so canst thou preach against no mischief except thou begin at the bishops."

### The meaning of the Gospel

[213] "The Gospel is everywhere one, though it be preached of diverse, and signifieth glad tidings: that is to wit, an open preaching of Christ, and the holy testament and gracious promises that God hath made in Christ's blood to all that repent and believe. Now [214] is there more gospel in one epistle of Paul, that is to say, Christ is more clearly preached and more promises rehearsed in one epistle of Paul, than in the three first evangelists, Matthew, Mark, and Luke."

## Superstitious gestures

[226] "What helpeth it also that the priest, when he goeth to mass, disguiseth himself with a great part of the passion of Christ, and playeth out the rest under silence, with signs and proffers, with nodding, becking and mowing, as it were jackanapes, when neither he himself neither any man else wotteth what he meaneth? Not at all, verily, but hurteth, and that exceedingly, forasmuch as it not only destroyeth the faith, and quencheth the love that should be given unto the commandments, and maketh the people unthankful, in that it bringeth them into such superstition that they think [227] that they have done abundantly enough for God, yea, and deserved above measure, if they be present once in a day at such mumming."

## Excessive wealth of the clergy

[236] "First, by the authority of the gospel, they that preach the word of God in every parish, and other necessary ministers, have right to challenge an honest living like unto one of the brethren, and therewith ought to be content. Bishops and priests that preach not, or that preach aught save God's word, are none of Christ's, nor of his anointing, but servants of the beast, whose mark they bear, whose word they preach, whose law they maintain clean against God's law, and with their false sophistry give him greater power than God ever gave to his Son Christ.

But they, as unsatiable beasts, not unmindful why they were shaven and shorn, because they will stand at no man's grace, or be in any man's danger, have gotten into their own hands, first the tithe or tenth of all the realm; then, I suppose, within a little or altogether, the third foot of all the temporal lands. Mark well how many parsonages or vicarages are there in the realm, which at the least have a plow-land apiece. Then note the lands of bishops, abbots, priors, nuns, knights of St. John's, cathedral churches, colleges, chantries, and free chapels. . ."

[238] "Last of all, what swarms of begging friars are there! The parson sheareth, the vicar shaveth, the parish priest polleth, the friar scrapeth, and the pardoner pareth: we lack but a butcher to pull off the skin."

**Vestments and titles**

[246] "Behold the monsters, how they are disguised with mitres, crosiers, and hats, with crosses, pillars, and poleaxes, and with three crowns! What names have they? My lord prior, my lord abbot, my lord bishop, my lord archbishop, cardinal, and legate; if it please your fatherhood; if it please your lordship; if it please your grace; if it like your holiness; and innumerable such like. Behold how they are esteemed, and how high they be crept up above all; not into worldly seats only, but into the seat of God, the hearts of men, where they sit above God himself."

[252] "Is not that shepherd's hook, the bishop's crose [= crosier], a false sign? Is not that white rochet, that the bishops and canons wear so like a nun, and so effeminately, a false sign? What other things are their sandals, gloves, mitres, and all the whole pomp of their disguising, than false signs, in which Paul prophesied that they should come? And as Christ warned us to beware of wolves in lambs' skins, and bade us look

rather unto their fruits and deeds than to wonder at their disguisings, run throughout all our holy religions, and thou shalt find them likewise all clothed in falsehood."

### The seal of the Holy Spirit upon a true minister of Christ

[254] "Subdeacon, deacon, priest, bishop, cardinal, patriarch, and pope, be names of offices and service, or should be, and not [255] sacraments. There is no promise coupled therewith. If they minister their offices truly, it is a sign that Christ's Spirit is in them; if not, that the devil is in them. Are these all sacraments, or which one of them? Or what thing in them is that holy sign or sacrament? The shaving, or the anointing? What also is the promise that is signified thereby? But what word printeth in them that character, that spiritual seal? O dreamers and natural beasts, without the seal of the Spirit of God, but sealed with the mark of the beast and with cankered consciences!

### The meaning of priesthood

There is a word called in Latin *sacerdos*, in Greek *hiereus*, in Hebrew *cohan*, that is, a minister, an officer, a sacrificer or a priest: as Aaron was a priest, and sacrificed for the people, and was a mediator between God and them. And in the English should it have had some other name than priest. But Antichrist hath deceived us with unknown and strange terms, to bring us into confusion and superstitious blindness. Of that manner is Christ a priest for ever, and all we priests through him, and need no more of any such priest on earth, to be a mean for us unto God. For Christ [256] hath brought us all into the inner temple, within the veil or forehanging, and unto the mercy-stool of God, and hath coupled us unto God, where we offer, every man for himself, the desires and petitions of his heart, and sacrifice and kill the lusts and appetites of his flesh, with prayer, fasting, and all manner godly living.

## The teaching ministry of an elder

Another word is there in Greek, called *presbyter*, in Latin *senior*, in English an *elder*, and is nothing but an officer to teach, and not to be a mediator between God and us. This need[eth] no anointing of man. They of the Old Testament were anointed with oil, to signify the anointing of Christ, and of us through Christ, with the Holy Ghost. Thiswise is no man priest, but he that is chosen, save as in time of necessity every person christeneth, so may every man teach his wife and household, and the wife her children. So in time of need, if I see my brother sin, I may between him and me rebuke him, and damn his deed by the law of God, and may also comfort them that are in despair, with the promises of God, and save them if they believe.

By a priest then, in the New Testament, understand nothing but an elder to teach the younger, and to bring them unto the full knowledge and understanding of Christ, and to minister the sacraments which Christ ordained, which is also [257] nothing but to preach Christ's promises. And by them that give all their study to quench the light of truth, and to hold the people in darkness, understand the disciples of Satan and messengers of Antichrist, whatsoever names they have, or whatsoever they call themselves."

## The prayer of a layman no less effectual than the prayer of a prelate

[258] "Nevertheless the truth is that we are all equally beloved in Christ, and God hath sworn to all indifferently. According therefore as every man believeth God's promises, longeth for them, and is diligent to pray unto God to fulfil them, so is his prayer heard. And as good is the prayer of a cobbler as of a cardinal, and of a butcher as of a bishop. And the blessing of a baker that knoweth the truth is as good as the blessing of our most holy father the pope. And by blessing understand not the wagging of the pope's or bishop's hand over thine head, but prayer: as when we say, 'God make thee a good man,' 'Christ put his Spirit in thee,' or 'Give thee grace and power to walk in the truth, and to follow his commandments,' etc."

## Priests not made by human ceremonies, but by Christ's command

"Last of all, one singular doubt they have: what maketh the priest? The anointing, or putting on of the hands, or what other ceremony, or what words? About which they brawl and scold, one ready to tear out another's throat. One saith this, and another that, but cannot agree. Neither can any of them make so strong a reason which another cannot improve, for they are all out of the way, and without the Spirit of God to judge spiritual things. Howbeit to this I answer, that when Christ called twelve up into the mountain and chose them, then immediately, without any anointing or ceremony, were they his apostles, that is to wit, ministers chosen to be sent to preach his testament unto all the whole world. And after the resurrection, when he had opened their wits and given them knowledge, to understand the secrets of his testament, and how to bind and loose, and what he would have them to do in all things, then he sent them forth with [259] a commandment to preach, and bind the unbelieving that continue in sin, and to loose the believing that repent. And that commandment, or charge, made them bishops, priests, popes, and all thing. . ."

"And (Acts vi) when the disciples that believed had chosen six deacons to minister to the widows, the apostles prayed and put their hands on them, and admitted them without more ado. Their putting on of hands was not after the manner of the dumb blessing of our holy bishops, with two fingers, but they spake unto them and told them their duty, and gave them a charge, and warned them to be faithful in the Lord's business: as we choose temporal officers and read their duty to them, and they promise to be faithful ministers and then are admitted. Neither is there any other manner or ceremony at all required in making of our spiritual officers, than to choose an able person and then to rehearse him his duty, and give him his charge, and so to put him in his room."

### Preacher to be chosen by the congregation

[283] "'By this means thou wilt that every man be a preacher,' will they say. Nay, verily. For God will that not, and therefore will I it not, no more than I

would that every man of London were mayor of London, or every man of the realm king thereof. God is not the author of dissension and strife, but of unity and peace, and of good order. I will therefore, that where a congregation is gathered together in Christ, one be chosen after the rule of Paul, and that he only preach, and else no man openly, but that every man teach his household after the same doctrine. But if the preacher preach false, then whosoever's heart God moveth, to the same it shall be lawful to rebuke and improve the false teacher with the clear and manifest scripture, and that same is no doubt a true prophet sent of God. For the scripture is God's, and theirs that believe, and not the false prophet's."

### The greed of false preachers

[300] "'They [i.e. the friars] preach,' sayest thou, 'and labour in the word.' First I say they are not called, and therefore ought not, for it is the curate's office. 'The curate cannot,' sayest thou. What doth the thief there then? Secondarily a true preacher preacheth Christ's testament only, and maketh Christ the cause and reward of all our deeds, and teacheth every man to bear his cross willingly for Christ's sake. But these are enemies unto the cross of Christ, and preach their belly, which is their god. . . Their longing is to fill their paunch, whom they serve, and not Christ; and through sweet preaching, and flattering words, deceive the hearts of the simple and unlearned."

[302] "The spiritualty increaseth daily. More prelates, more priests, more monks, friars, canons, nuns, and more heretics (I would say heremites), with

like draff. Set before thee the increase of St. Francis' disciples in so few years. Reckon how many thousand, yea, how many twenty thousands, not disciples only, but whole cloisters, are sprung out of hell of them in so little space. Pattering of prayers increaseth daily. Their service, as they call it, waxeth longer and longer, and the labour of their lips greater; new saints, new service, new feasts, and new holy days. What take all these away? Sin? Nay, for we see the contrary by experience, and that sin groweth as they grow. But they take away first God's word, with faith, hope, peace, unity, love and concord, then house and land, rent and fee, tower and town, goods and [303] cattle, and the very meat out of men's mouths. All these live by purgatory. When other weep for their friends, they sing merrily; when other lose their friends, they get friends.

The pope, with all his pardons, is grounded on purgatory. Priests, monks, canons, friars, with all other swarms of hypocrites, do but empty purgatory and fill hell. 'Every mass,' say they, 'delivereth one soul out of purgatory.' If that were true, yea, if ten masses were enough for one soul, yet were the parish priests and curates of every parish sufficient to scour purgatory: all the other costly workmen might be well spared."

### The preacher's use of allegories and similitudes

[312] "And as I have said of allegories, even so it is of worldly similitudes, which we make either when we preach, either when we expound the scripture. The similitudes prove nothing, but are made to express more plainly that which is contained in the scripture,

and to lead thee in the spiritual understanding of the text: as the similitude of matrimony is taken to express the marriage that is between Christ and our souls, and what exceeding mercy we have there, whereof all the scriptures make mention. And the similitude of the members, how every one of them careth for other, is taken to make thee feel what it is to love thy neighbour as thyself. That preacher therefore, that bringeth a naked similitude to prove that which is contained in no text of scripture, nor followeth of a text, count a deceiver, a leader out of the way, and a false prophet, and beware of his philosophy and persuasions of man's wisdom, as Paul everywhere warneth thee."

### A priest must abide by the law

[333] "I proved also that all men, without exception, are under the temporal sword, whatsoever names they give themselves. Because the priest is chosen out of the laymen to teach this obedience, is that a lawful cause for him to disobey? Because he preacheth that the layman should not steal, is it therefore lawful for him to steal unpunished? Because thou teachest me that I may not kill, or if I do, the king must kill me again, is it therefore lawful for thee to kill and go free? Other [= Or] whether is it rather meet that thou, which art my guide to teach me the right way, shouldest walk therein before me?

The priests of the old law with their high bishop Aaron, and all his successors, though they were anointed by God's commandment, and appointed to serve God in his temple, and exempt from all offices and ministering of worldly matters, were yet nevertheless under the temporal sword, if they brake the laws. Christ saith to Peter, 'All that take the sword shall perish by the sword.' Here is none exception. Paul saith, 'All souls must obey'. Here is none exception. Paul himself is here not exempt. God saith (Genesis ix), 'Whosoever sheddeth man's blood, by man shall his blood be shed again.' Here is nonc exception.

Moreover Christ became poor, to make other men rich; and bound, to make others free. He left also with his disciples the law of love. Now love seeketh not her own profit, but her neighbour's; love seeketh not her own freedom, but becometh surety and bond to make her neighbour free. Damned therefore are the spiritualty by all the laws of God, which through falsehood and disguised hypocrisy have sought so great profit, so great riches, so great authority, and so great liberties, and have so beggared the lay, and so brought them in subjection and bondage, and so despised them, that they have set up franchises [= places of sanctuary] in all towns and villages, for whosoever robbeth, murdereth, or slayeth them, and even for traitors unto the king's person also."

---

*The Practice of Prelates* (1530)

---

**Violent rule exercised by the clergy**

[II. 249] "The world truly can see no other way to rule than with violence, for there no man abstaineth from evil, but for fear, because the love of righteousness is not written in their hearts. And therefore the pope's kingdom is of the world, for there one sort are your grace, your holiness, your fatherhood; another, my lord bishop, my lord abbot, my lord prior; another, master doctor, father, bachelor, master parson, master vicar; and at the last cometh in simple sir John. And every man reigneth over other with might, and have every ruler his prison, his jailor, his chains, his torments, even so much as the friars Observants observe that rule, and compel every man other with violence above the cruelness of the heathen tyrants, so that what cometh once in may never out, for fear of telling tales out of school. They rule over the body with violence, and compel it, whether the heart will or not, to observe things of their own making."

**The rule of scripture**

[251] "So now thou seest that in the kingdom of Christ, and in his church or congregation, and in his councils, the ruler is the scripture, approved through the miracles of the Holy Ghost, and men be servants only, and Christ is the head, and we all brethren. And when we call men our heads, that we do, not because they be shorn or shaven, or because of their names, parson, vicar, bishop, pope, but only because of the word which they preach. If they err from the word, then may whosoever God moveth his heart, play Paul, and correct him. If he will not obey the scripture, then have his brethren authority by the scripture to put him down, and to send him out of Christ's church among the heretics, which prefer their false doctrine above the true word of Christ."

## The preaching of the pope

[274] "And the pope, after he had received the kingdom of the world of the devil, and was become the devil's vicar, took up in like manner all Christendom on high, and brought them from the meekness of Christ unto the high hill of the pride of Lucifer, and shewed them all the kingdoms of the earth, saying, 'Fall down and worship me, and I will give you these.' Unto the spiritualty he saith, 'Fall from Christ, and [275] preach me, and take thou that cardinalship, thou that bishopric, thou that abbotship, and so forth, thou as many benefices as thou wilt, and a dispensation for what thou wilt.' And to monks and friars in like manner: 'Take thou that hole, and thou that nest, with what privileges ye will desire, and dispensations of your rules, if ye will preach me.'"

"The apostles chose priests to preach Christ only, all other things laid apart, and chose none but learned and virtuous. The pope shaveth whosoever cometh... and when they be sworn, he sendeth them unto all great men's houses to preach his godhead, to be stewards, surveyors, receivers, and counsellors of all manner mischief: to corrupt wife, daughter, and maid, and to betray their own master..."

## Deacons and subdeacons

"The apostles chose deacons to minister the alms of the [276] rich unto the poor... And instead of such deacons he [i.e. the pope] maketh both deacons and subdeacons, which do nothing at all but are vain names without office, except it be that on some holy day, instead of ministering the goods of the church unto the poor, they sing an epistle or gospel, to beg more from the poor."

### Paying for priests who do not preach

[288] "And where, before God, no man is a priest but he that is appointed to preach Christ's Gospel unto the people; and the people ought not to give aught unto the spiritualty, but for the maintenance of the preaching of God's word; the pope taketh six or seven, yea, ten, twenty, and as many benefices as he listeth, and giveth them unto one that preacheth not at all, as he doth all other dignities of the spiritualty. He that will purchase, and pay, and be sworn, shall have what he will."

### Elaborate services and ceremonies a hindrance to true faith

[290] "And thus, because that the scripture would not agree with them, they thrust it out of the way first, and shut up the kingdom of heaven, which is Christ's Gospel, with false expositions, and with such sophistry, and with false principles of natural wisdom. And the abbots took the scripture from their monks, lest some should ever bark against the abbots' living; and set up such long service and singing, to weary them withal, that they should have no leisure to read in the scripture but with their lips; and made them good cheer to fill their bellies, and to stop their mouths. And the bishops in like manner, to occupy their priests withal, that they should not study the scripture for barking against them,

set up long service, wondrous intricate, so that in a dozen years thou couldst scarce learn to turn aright unto it: long matins, [291] long evensongs, long masses, long *diriges*, with vantage yet to mitigate the tediousness, *quia levis est labor cum lucro*, for 'lucre' (say they) 'maketh the labour light': ever noselling [= nurturing] them in ceremonies, and in their own constitutions, decrees, ordinances, and laws of holy church."

### The false principles of university teaching

"And in the universities they have ordained that no man shall look on the scripture until he be noselled [= nurtured] in heathen learning eight or nine years, and armed with false principles, with which he is clean shut out of the understanding of the scripture. And at his first coming unto the university he is sworn that he shall not defame the university, whatsoever he seeth. And when he taketh first degree, he is sworn that he shall hold none opinion condemned by the church, but what such opinions be, that he shall not know.

And then, when they be admitted unto [= to] study divinity, because the scripture is locked up with such false expositions, and with false principles of natural philosophy, that they cannot enter in, they go about the outside and dispute all their lives about words and vain opinions, pertaining as much unto the healing of a man's heel, as health of his soul: provided yet alway, lest God give his singular grace unto any person, that none may preach except he be admitted of the bishops."

*An Answer unto Sir Thomas More's Dialogue* (1531)

## Women's ministry

[III. 18] "Women be no meet vessels to rule or to preach, for both are forbidden them, yet hath God endoted [= endowed] them with his Spirit at sundry times, and shewed his power [and] goodness upon them, and wrought wonderful things by them, because he would not have them despised. We read that women have judged all Israel, and have been great prophetesses, and have done mighty deeds. Yea, and if stories be true, women have preached since the opening of the New Testament. Do not our women now christen and minister the sacrament of baptism in time of need? Might they not, by as good reason, preach also, if necessity required? If a woman were driven into some island, where Christ was never preached, might she there not preach him, if she had the gift thereto? Might she not also baptize? And why might she not, by the same reason, minister the sacrament of the body and blood of Christ, and teach them how to choose officers and ministers? O poor women, how despise ye them! . . . Notwithstanding, though God be under no law, and necessity lawless, yet be we under a law, and ought to prefer the men before the women, and age before youth, as nigh as we can. For it is against the law of nature that young men should rule the elder, and as uncomely as that women should rule the men, but when need requireth."

### Ignorance of the Lord's Prayer

[75] "Yea, and I dare say that there be twenty thousand priests, curates, this day in England, and not so few, that cannot give you the right English unto this text in the Paternoster, *Fiat voluntas tua, sicut in coelo et in terra*, and answer thereto."

### The avoidance of superstition regarding the Sabbath

[97] "And as for the Sabbath, a great matter, we be lords over the Sabbath, and may yet change it into the Monday, or any other day, as we see need, or may make every tenth day holy day only, if we see a cause why. We may make two every week, if it were expedient, and one not enough to teach the people. Neither was there any cause to change it from the Saturday, than to put difference between us and the Jews, and lest we should become servants unto the day, after their superstition. Neither needed we any holy day at all, if the people might be taught without it."

---

*An Exposition upon the fifth, sixth, and seventh chapters of Matthew* (1533?)

---

### True preaching as "salting"

[II. 31] "The office of an apostle and true preacher is to salt, not only the corrupt manners and conversation of earthy [= earthly] people, but also the rotten heart within, and all that springeth out thereof: their natural reason, their will, their understanding and wisdom, yea, and their faith and belief, and all that they have imagined without God's word, concerning righteousness, justifying, satisfaction, and serving of God. And the nature of salt is to bite, fret, and make smart.

And the sick patients of the world are marvellous impatient, so that though with great pain they can suffer their gross sins to be rebuked under a fashion, as in a parable afar off, yet, to have their righteousness, their holiness, and serving of God and his saints, disallowed, improved, and condemned for damnable and devilish, that may they not abide. Insomuch that thou [32] must leave thy salting or else be prepared to suffer again, even to be called a railer, seditious, a maker of discord, and a troubler of the common peace, yea, a schismatic, and an heretic also, and to be lied upon, that thou hast done and said that thou never thoughtest, and then to be called *coram nobis* [i.e. into the presence of a judge], and to sing a new song, and forswear salting, or else to be sent after thy fellows that are gone before, and the way thy Master went.

True preaching is a salting that stirreth up persecution, and an office that no man is meet for, save he that is seasoned himself before with poverty in spirit, softness, meekness, patience, mercifulness, pureness of heart, and hunger of righteousness, and looking for persecution too, and hath all his hope, comfort, and solace, in the blessing only, and in no worldly thing.

'Nay,' will some say, 'a man might preach long enough without persecution, yea, and get favour too, if he would not meddle with the pope, bishops, prelates, and holy ghostly people that live in contemplation and solitariness, nor with great men of the world.' I answer, true preaching is salting, and all that is corrupt must be salted. And those persons are of all other most corrupt, and therefore may not be left untouched.

The pope's pardons must be rebuked. The abuse of the mass, of the sacraments, and of all the ceremonies must be rebuked and salted. And selling of merits and of prayers must be salted. The abuse of fasting and of pilgrimage must be salted. All idolatry and false faith must be rebuked. And those friars that teach men to believe in St. Francis' coat, how that they shall never come in hell or purgatory if they be buried therein, may not be passed over with silence. . ."

[33] "'If salt have lost his saltness, it is good for nothing but to be trodden underfoot of men.' That is, if the preacher, which for his doctrine is called salt, have lost the nature of salt, that is to say, his sharpness in rebuking all unrighteousness, all natural reason, natural wit, and understanding, and all trust and confidence in whatsoever it be, save in the blood of Christ: he is condemned of God, and disallowed of all them that cleave to the truth. In what case stand they then that have benefices and preach not? Verily though they stand at the altar, yet are they excommunicate and cast out of the living church of almighty God. . ."

### The preacher and the layman

[36]"'Every man then may be a common preacher,' thou wilt say, 'and preach everywhere by his own authority.' Nay verily, no man may yet be a common preacher save he that is called and chosen thereto by the common ordinance of the congregation, as long as

the preacher teacheth the true word of God. But every private man ought to be, in virtuous living, both light and salt to his neighbour, insomuch that the poorest ought to strive to overrun the bishop, and to preach to him in example of living. Moreover, every man ought to preach in word and deed unto his household, and to them that are under his governance, etc.

And though no man may preach openly, save he that hath the office committed unto him, yet ought every man to endeavour himself to be as well learned as the preacher, as nigh as it is possible. And every man may privately inform his neighbour, yea, and the preacher and bishop too, if need be. For if the preacher preach wrong, then may any man, whatsoever he be, rebuke him, first privately, and then if that help not, to complain further. And when all is proved, according to the order of charity, and yet none amendment had, then ought every man that can to resist him, and to stand by Christ's doctrine, and to jeopard life and all for it. Look on the old examples and they shall teach thee."

---

*Prologue to the 1534 New Testament*

---

**Elders or priests, servants of the word of God**

[I. 478] "In the Old Testament the temporal heads and rulers of the Jews, which had the governance over the lay or common people, are called elders, as ye may see in the four evangelists. Out of which custom Paul in his epistle, and also Peter, call the prelates and spiritual governors, which are bishops and priests, ‘elders’. Now, whether ye call them elders or priests, it is to me all one, so that ye understand that they be officers and servants of the word of God: unto the which all men, both high and low, that will not rebel against Christ, must obey, as long as they preach and rule truly, and no longer.”

# ABBREVIATIONS

| | |
|---|---|
| Anderson | C. Anderson *The Annals of the English Bible* (2 vols., 1845) |
| Boase | C. W. Boase *Register of the University of Oxford,* i (Oxford, 1885) |
| Campbell | W. E. Campbell *Erasmus, Tyndale and More* (1949) |
| Daniell | D. Daniell *William Tyndale, A Biography* (1994) |
| Demaus | R. Demaus *William Tindale, A Biography* (1871) |
| Demaus-Lovett *1886* | ——— revised by R. Lovett (1886) |
| Demaus-Lovett *1904* | ——— ——— (1904) |
| Foxe | J. Foxe *Acts and Monuments* ed. G. Townsend (8 vols., 1843-9) |
| Foxe *1559* | ——— *Rerum in Ecclesia Gestarum. . . Commentaria* (Basle, 1559) |
| Foxe *1563* | ——— *Actes and Monuments* (1563) |
| Foxe *1570* | ——— ——— (2 vols., 1570) |
| Greenfield | B. W. Greenfield *Notes Relating to the Family of Tyndale* (1878) |
| *LP* | *Letters and Papers, Foreign and Domestic, of the Reign of Henry VIII* ed. J. S. Brewer *et al.* (21 vols., 1862-1932) |
| Mozley | J. F. Mozley *William Tyndale* (1937) |
| Offor | G. Offor *Memoir of William Tyndale* (1836) |
| PRO | Public Record Office |
| Walter | [Collected Works of Tyndale] ed. H. Walter (Parker Society, 3 vols., 1848-50) |
| Williams | C. H. Williams *William Tyndale* (1969) |

# NOTES

1. E. Halle *The Vnion of the two noble and illustrate famelies of Lancastre and Yorke* (1548), f. 227r; Foxe *1559*, 138; Foxe *1563*, 520; Foxe *1570* (ii). 1224; id. *The Whole Workes of W. Tyndall, Iohn Frith, and Doct. Barnes* (1572-3), sig. A.iii.r. For the full narrative of Halle and Foxe, see pp. 36-41 below.

2. In this study, the pre-1974 county names will be used. It should be noted that from 1536 onwards, Monmouthshire was often treated as an English county. It was certainly regarded as a border region. However, at the time of Tyndale's birth, Monmouthshire was indisputably a part of Wales. When Halle said that England was Tyndale's "native country", and John Bale described him as an "Englishman" (*Anglus* 1548; omitted in 1557 - see p. 39), this would have been a misleading way of describing someone born in 15th-century Monmouthshire. Nevertheless J. F. Mozley, a prominent biographer of Tyndale, once expressed the opinion that this was the county of Tyndale's birth: see Campbell 97. As will be seen later, there is another area which may have a stronger claim to this privilege.

3. R. Atkyns *The Ancient and Present State of Glostershire* (1712), 579; Greenfield 2-7; Anderson i. 16-22; Mozley 1-7; Daniell 9-12.

4. Greenfield 7, 8, 13; Demaus-Lovett 22; Mozley 2-3; Daniell 10.

5. PRO, SP1/74, f. 94r; *LP* vi. 82.

6. *LP* iii (i). 405.

7. See note 9 below.

8. Cf. C. Overy and A. C. Tyndale "The Parentage of William Tyndale, *alias* Huchyns, Translator and Martyr" *Transactions of the Bristol and Gloucestershire Archaeological Society* lxxiii (1954), 212-13. However, there is rather less evidence for their further contention that William Tyndale is to be identified with a person of that name who in 1507 was joint tenant of Melksham Court near Stinchcombe.

9. PRO, C82/440; *LP* ii (i). 2570; cf. Demaus-Lovett *1904*, 22-5, Mozley 3-5, Daniell 10-11.

10. Mozley 21; cf. J. F. Mozley "The Life of Tyndale" *Tyndale Commemoration Volume* (1939), 224.

11. A. T. Bannister *Registrum Ricardi Mayew, Episcopi Herefordensis* (Cantilupe Society, 1919; Canterbury and York Society, xxvii, 1921), 266, 290.

12. Cf. Williams 2, 6; Daniell 56.

13. London, Guildhall Library, MS 9531/8, f. 85r; cf. Offor 7-8. The same Tyndale had been ordained as subdeacon on 24 September 1502, and deacon on 17 December 1502 (MS 9531/8, ff. 83v, 84r).

14. Offor 8; W. S. Simpson *Gleanings From Old St. Paul's* (1889), 44; id. *St. Paul's Cathedral Library* (1893), 68.

15. Demaus 35-7; Demaus-Lovett *1904*, 57-8.

16. Mozley 21; Greenfield 7.

17. Mozley's conjecture that Tyndale's ordination as priest was "about 1515" is thereby proved correct. See Campbell 102.

18. Boase ix-x, 80.

19. T. More *The confutacyon of Tyndales answere* (1532), cliii.

20. See pp. 57, 64.

21. Lincoln, Lincolnshire Archives Office, *Episcopal Register* xxv, ff. 111v, 112r, 113v.

22. Cf. Erasmus *Opus Epistolarum* ed. P. S. Allen *et al.* (Oxford, 1906-58) ii. 37; iv. 524.

23. J. Colet *Oratio habita a D. Ioanne Colet Decano Sancti Pauli ad Clerum in Conuocatione M.D.xj* [sic] (c. 1512 = STC 5545), sig. B.iii.v.; *The sermon of doctor Colete made to the Conuocacion at Paulis* (1530 = STC 5550), sig. B.viii.v.

24. For a good account of this episode, see W. R. Cooper "Richard Hunne" *Reformation* i (1996), 221-51.

25. Cf. pp. 60-1.

26. R. W. Hoyle *The Military Survey of Gloucestershire, 1522* (Bristol and Gloucestershire Archaeological Society, 1993), 67.

27. M. A. Faraday and E. J. L. Cole edd. *Calendar of Probate and Administrative Acts. . .in the Court Books of the Bishop of Hereford* (1989), items 53/331, 72/208, 86/348, 90/166, 94/210. A John and Robert "Hiches" also appear in a court roll for the Bledisloe Hundred in 1445: Gloucestershire Record Office, MS D421/M13.

28. A. T. Bannister ed. *The Register of John Stanbury, Bishop of Hereford* (Cantilupe Society, 1918; Canterbury and York Society, xxv, 1919), 118-25; id. ed. *Registrum Ricardi Mayew, Episcopi Herefordensis* (Cantilupe Society, 1919; Canterbury and York Society, xxvii, 1921), 109-10; J. A. F. Thomson *The Later Lollards, 1414-1520* (Oxford, 1965), 40-2, 47-8.

29. For a discussion of Lollard elements in Tyndale's theology, see D. D. Smeeton *Lollard Themes in the Reformation Theology of William Tyndale* (Sixteenth Century Essays and Studies, vi, Kirksville, Missouri, 1986).

30. Demaus-Lovett *1904*, 22; Mozley 121-2, 170-1; Daniell 180-1.

31. A. T. Bannister ed. *Registrum Caroli Bothe, Episcopi Herefordensis* (Cantilupe Society, 1921; Canterbury and York Society, xxviii, 1921), 304-5.

32. Offor 7; Anderson i. 21; Walter i. xiv; Demaus 9.

33. Demaus-Lovett *1886*, 8 (citing Boase).

34. Mozley 1, 13.

35. Campbell 97, 102.

36. See especially *The History of the University of Oxford*, vols. ii-iii (Oxford, 1992, 1986), and Daniell 22-48.

37. Mozley 12; Daniell 28.

38. Boase ix-x; Demaus-Lovett *1886*, 3-4, reproducing Boase's material. The same information is found in S. L. Greenslade *The Work of William Tindale* (1938), 3.

39. The following explanations of technical terms are dependent on the explanations found in A. Clark *Register of the University of Oxford* ii (i) (Oxford, 1887), 1-107, and J. M. Fletcher "Developments in the Faculty of Arts 1370-1520" in *The History of the University of Oxford*, ii (Oxford, 1992), 315-45.

40. See pp. 40-1, below.

41. See R. S. Stanier *Magdalen School. A History of Magdalen College School, Oxford* (Oxford, 1958), 66-7; Daniell 22-7.

42. Demaus-Lovett *1904*, 35-6; Mozley 12-13; Daniell 10, 22, 28.

43. See pp. 38-40.

44. Mozley vii.

45. Foxe iv. 617; Foxe *1559*, 128; Foxe *1563*, 497; Foxe *1570* (ii). 1133; cf. Demaus-Lovett *1904*, 56. In effect, Foxe deleted Tyndale's name from one passage, but reintroduced it into another, in his 1570 edition. His error resulted in continuing confusion on this point among Tyndale's later biographers.

46. Tyndale's translation of Ezra and Nehemiah, if it ever existed, no longer survives.

47. Some of these passages of Tyndale's writings are usefully discussed in Smeeton (*op. cit.*, n. 29), 159-220.

# INDEX


Aaron 54, 60
Abbots 53, 62-4
Acon. *See* St. Thomas the Martyr
Alms 63-4
Anderson, C. 24
Anointing 52, 54-7, 60
Antichrist(s) 39-40, 47, 51, 54, 56
Antwerp 38
Appulby, Thomas 31
Archbishops 53
Aristotle 48
Assumption of Mary 49
Assurance 44
Atkyns, Robert 73
Awre 22
Aylburton 22

Balaamites 39-40
Bale, John 35, 39-40, 73
Bannister, A. T. 12
Bead-roll 47
Berkeley 9-10
Bible
- corrupted by "doctors" 49
- knowledge of 45
- reading in English 23, 45-6
- teaching 47-8
- as the rule of faith 62
- kept from monks 64

Bishops
- as Antichrist 51, 54
- as elders 71
- failure to preach 52
- false preachers 63
- garments of 53
- hostility to Bible 64-5
- hostility to true preaching 51
- involvement in government 45
- manner of blessing 56-7
- prayers of 56
- servants of Devil 52
- titles 62
- to be rebuked 51, 68
- worldliness 20, 45, 51, 53

Bledisloe Hundred 74
Blessing 56-7
Blunstone, Richard 31
Boase, C. W. 26, 75
Bothe, Charles (bp. of Hereford) 75
Brabant 37
Brussels 37

Cambridge University 41
Canon law 65
Canonical age 25
Canons 53, 58-9
Cardinal College, Oxford 35
Cardinals 53-4, 56, 63
Carlisle, diocese 15
Cathedrals 53
Ceremonies 33, 47, 56-7, 65, 69
Chantries 53
Character, clerical 54
Cheshire 8
Christening 55, 66
Clergy
- corrupting influence of 63
- criminality 60
- do not understand Latin 46
- failure to preach 44-6, 52, 64, 69
- false preachers 46-7, 60, 64
- flatterers 58
- greed 46, 52-3, 58-9, 61
- non-residence 46-7
- oppressive to the laity 61-2
- pluralism 47, 63-4
- preaching the papacy 63
- pride 53
- servants of the Devil 47, 52, 55-6
- worldliness 53, 63

Colet, John (dean of St. Paul's) 20-1
Collegiate churches 53
Confession 23, 47
Congregation 42, 69
Convocation, of clergy 20
Cornyshe, John 31
Cromwell, Thomas 10, 39
Crosiers 53
Crosses 53
Curates (or parish priests) 43, 45-7, 53, 58-9, 62, 67

Deacons 15-20, 54, 57, 64
Demaus, R. 15, 24
Devil, the 50, 52, 54-5, 63
- *See also* Antichrist

Dirige-money 47
Dispensations, papal 25, 63
Dunstable 20

Education, theological 42, 48-9, 65
Elders 55, 70-1

Election, doctrine of
44-5
Ely, diocese 15
Eternal life 44
Excommunication
70

Faith 44-5, 48, 51-2,
55-7, 59, 68-9
Falowfylde, John 31
Fasting 55, 69
Female ministry
42, 55, 66
Fitzjames, Richard
(bp. of London)
16-17, 20-1
Foxe, John
8, 34-36, 40-1, 73
Franciscan friars 59
Free chapels 53
Friars 15, 49-50, 53,
58-9, 62-3, 69

Gallipoli, suffragan
bishopric 16-17
Gloucestershire
8-11, 14, 22-3, 75
Gloves 53
Gospel
38, 43, 48, 51, 64
Grace, of God
44-5, 48, 65
Greenslade, S. L. 75
Greenwich Observant,
friar 15

Halle, Edward
8, 34-5, 37-9, 73
Hats, of clergy 53
Hell 49, 59, 69
Heochyns
*See* Hychyns
Hereford, diocese
12-14, 16-18, 21-4,
35
Herefordshire
8, 12, 18, 22
Hiches, Hichyns, Ho-
chyns. *See* Hychyns
Holy days
45, 59, 63, 67
*See also* Sabbath
Holy Spirit 44-5, 48,
54-6, 62, 66
Horsey, William
(chancellor of
bp. of London) 21
Huchens. *See* Hychyns
Hunne, Richard 21
Hurst 10
Hutchins, Hycchyns
*See* Hychyns
Hychyns, William. *See*
Tyndale, William
Hychyns (Heochyns)
Richard (of Nass) 22
William (of Nass) 22
William (of Purton)
22
Hychyns (Hiches)
John 74
Robert 74
Hychyns, John
12-13, 23-4
Hychys. *See* Hychyns

Idolatry 50, 69
Indulgences 23

Justification 68

Knights of St. John 53

Law, of God
47-8, 52, 55-6, 66
*See also* Canon law
Laying on of hands
56-7
Laymen 45-6, 56, 70
Legates, papal 53
Letters dimissory
12, 14, 16-18
Limbo 49
Lincoln 20
Lincoln, diocese
15, 19-20
Little Sodbury 8
Lollards 21-3, 75
London. *See*
St. Mary Overie;
St. Paul's Cathedral;
St. Thomas the
Martyr
London, diocese 15-21
Louvain 37-8
Love 43-4, 47-8, 52,
56, 59-62
Lovett, R. 24, 26
Lucifer. *See* Devil
Ludlow 24
Luther, influence of
7, 20, 33, 38
Lydney 22-3

Magdalen College,
Oxford 34, 41
Magdalen College
School, Oxford 34-6
Magdalen Hall, Oxford
34, 41
Mark of the Beast
50, 54
Mary, the Virgin 49
Mass 16, 32-3, 46, 52,
59, 65, 69. *See also*
Transubstantiation
Mass-penny 47
Mayew, Richard (bp. of
Hereford) 12-14, 23
Melksham Court 73
Merits, sale of 69
Micheldean 23
Mitres 53
Monks 50-1, 58-9, 63-4
Monmouthshire 11, 73
More, Sir Thomas 18
Mozley, J. F.
12, 14, 24, 35, 73-4

Nass 22
Newnham 22
Nibley 9
Nibley Knoll 9, 22
Nuns 53, 58

Oaths, swearing of
51, 63-5

Obedience
47, 50-1, 60, 71
Observant friars 15, 62
Offor, George 24
Ordination 12-20, 23-5, 42, 54, 56-7
Original sin 47, 49
Oxford University
15, 18-19, 26-35, 38-41, 48-9, 65

Pantrey, John 32
Pardoners 53
Pardons 59, 69
Parsons (or Rectors)
47, 53, 62
Patriarchs 54
Persecution 22-3, 68
Peterborough 20
Phillips, Henry 38
Pilgrimage 69
Pluralism 47, 63-4
Pope 38, 46-7, 50, 54, 56-7, 59, 62-4, 68-9
Prayer
23, 50, 55-6, 59, 69
Preachers
anointed 52, 55
assurance of salvation 44
character 63, 68
chosen
by congregation 42, 57-8, 69
by God 55, 57
conscious of unworthiness 44
Devil in 54
false preachers
to be expelled 62
to be rebuked 58, 62, 70
Holy Spirit in 44, 54
income 43, 52, 64
kept out by bishops 65
not mediators 55
not to alter the Word of God 43
of the Gospel 43
persecuted 68
to be learned 63
Preaching
against Antichrist 51
against bishops 51
against false doctrine 69
against unrighteousness 69
as "salting" 67-9
as duty of bishop 51
by women, exceptionally 66
commanded by Christ 42, 57
exposition of proverbs and similitudes 48, 59-60
for spiritual reward 43-4
necessity of 43-4
of God's promises 48, 51, 55
of Gospel 48, 51, 63-4
of the law 47-8
only by those who are called 58
out of love for God 44
teaching the Bible 48
to be judged by the Bible 48
to one's own household 70
willingly 44
with right motives 44
Presbyter. *See* Elders
Priesthood, of all Christians 42, 54
Priests
19, 52, 54-9, 64-5, 67, 70-1
*See also* Clergy
Priors 53, 62
Prisons, ecclesiastical 62
Profession, of monks 51
Promises, of God 48, 51, 54-6
Prophetesses 66
Prophets 58, 60
Proverbs, exposition of 48
Purgatory 23, 49, 59, 69
Purton 22-3

Repentance 51, 57
Righteousness 68
Rochet 53

Sabbath 67
Sacraments
48, 54-5, 66, 69
St. Francis 69
St. John the Baptist, hospital (Ludlow) 24
St. Mary Overie, priory (Southwark) 12-13, 16-18
St. Mary's, church (Oxford) 28
St. Paul's Cathedral (London) 15-16, 20
St. Thomas the Martyr of Acon, hospital (London) 17
Saints 50, 59, 68
Sandals 53
Satan. *See* Devil
Sects 49-50
Services of worship 59, 64-5. *See also* Mass
Shaving, of clergy 50, 52, 54, 62-3
Shelley, Thomas 30-1
Shropshire 8
"Sicientes" Saturday 16
Signs, false 53
Similitudes 48, 50, 60
Simony 64

Sin
44, 47, 49, 55, 57, 59
Slimbridge 9-10, 22
Southwark
*See* St. Mary Overie
Squere, Robert 30-1
Stanbury, John (bp. of Hereford) 74
Stevynson, John 30
Stinchcombe
9-10, 22, 73
Stokesley, John (bp. of London) 10
Subdeacons 12-13, 19, 23, 54, 63-4
Superstition 52, 54

Tendall. *See* Tyndale
Tewkesbury 10
Tindale. *See* Tyndale
Tithes 46-7
Titles, clerical 53, 62
Transubstantiation 23
Trentals 47
Tunstall, Cuthbert (as bp. of London) 19
Turks 46
Tyndale, Edward 10
Tyndale, John (brother of William) 23
Tyndale, William
academic disputations 27
anniversaries 7, 24
bachelor of arts
16-18, 25-30
Bible translator
7, 19, 35, 37-8
birth, date
15, 24-5, 34
birth, place 8-11, 14-15, 21-3, 37, 40-1
at Cambridge University 41
Cardinal College, Oxford, alleged membership of 35
character 37-41
death 7, 9, 37, 39
"determines" as B.A.
27-30
dispensations 30-3
earlier beliefs
7, 19
an "Englishman"
38-9, 73
as William Hychyns (Hichyns, Hochyns, Huchens, Hycchyns)
9, 12-18, 22, 26-7, 29-33, 37, 39
influence of Colet
20-1
influence of Lollards
21, 23
influence of Luther
7, 20, 33, 38
influence of Bible
7, 21, 34, 38, 41
lecturer 29
letters dimissory
12, 14, 16-18
London, visits
16-21
Magdalen College School, alleged attendance at
34, 37
Magdalen Hall, residence at
34, 41
master of arts
18, 26, 30-3
monument 9
ordination 11-25
at Oxford
15, 18, 26-41
reformer 7, 33
religious views
*See* under individual topics
upbringing 34-41
works
"An Answer unto Sir Thomas More's Dialogue" 66-7
"An Exposition of. . . Matthew"
67-70
Prologue to 1534 New Testament
70-1
"The Obedience of a Christian Man" 9, 45-61
"The Parable of the Wicked Mammon"
9, 43-5
"The Practice of Prelates" 61-5
Tyndale, William (others of this name)
9, 15, 73
Tyndale-Hychyns family
9, 22
Tyndall. *See* Tyndale

Vicars 47, 53, 62-3
Vilvorde 37
Vows 51

Wales 8, 10-11, 22, 37, 40-1, 73
Walsh, Sir John 8
Walter, H. 24
Warham, William (as bp. of London) 15
Whitborne 12-13, 23
Winchester, diocese
13, 15, 17
Woolaston 22-3
Worcester, diocese
14-15
Works, of man 45, 58
Wyclif, John
21, 23, 39-40

Young, John (suffragan bp. of Gallipoli)
16-17